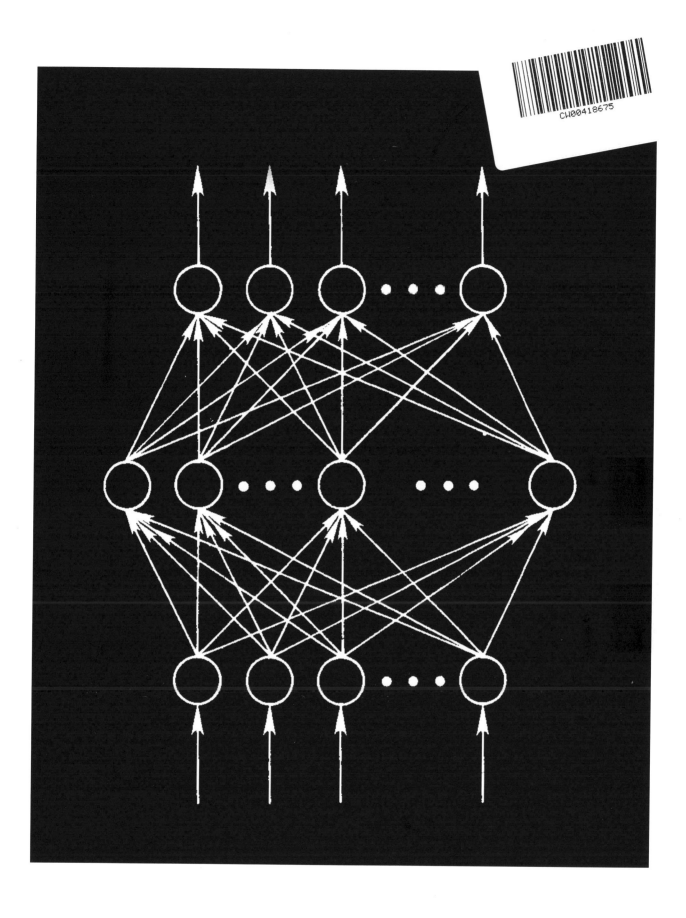

1

Instructions for use

The contents of this work emerge

from a broader scientific context than the neural one,

inside which conditions are being created

for a transition of knowledge

towards more complex explicative models.

Cognitive science is moving its focus

from the processing of abstract symbols

to the role of the body in cognition;

artificial intelligence starts experimenting semantic algorithms;

the internet of things strives for creating devices

able to automatically comprehend;

individual creativity is becoming more and more

collective intelligence.

In this field the self-generating neural networks

are speeding up the above-mentioned innovations,

leveraging some foundations of their own platform,

as described in this work:

- the automatic processes for information elaboration
- the sub-symbolic language of neural networks
- the self- generating processes of complex systems
- biopsychic collective intelligence
- the endogenous language of objects
- the scientific conception of creativity
  (art, design, exhibition systems and advertising)

ABSTRACT

In this work we present some innovative aspects
of the visual communication which have emerged
thanks to the use of neural networks.

The first innovation consists of
the identification of a "double code" implemented
in the expressive system of the art works:
underneath the stylistic, historical and cultural configuration
of a painting, sculpture, advertising, or exhibition set-up
acts a sub-symbolic hidden code
that releases biopsychic signals
able to increase the attractive power of the work.

The presence of such signals
has been found out in many masterpieces of great artists,
who have reached undisputable fame
in every age and place.
Let's think about Leonardo's Mona Lisa,
but many other works
by Renoir, Beuys, Magritte, Chagall,
Brewster, Cattelan, Quinn, Hirst and others.
But how could these artists invent
such sophisticated expressive systems?
The answer emerges from the processes of
"automatic elaboration"
of the sensations, intuitions and artists' nose,
which only today can be scientifically explained

by the neural networks modelling.

In other words these artists
have let themselves be guided
by the biological code of the expressive systems.

Thanks to the use of the same neural platform
further innovative aspects
have been discovered in the design field.
The design has therefore become
a self generating dynamic system
of many biopsychic functions
interconnected the ones with the others
in a network.
A chair conceived only to let people sit,
can't function well even for that!

Obviously, in this new research perspective
also the design as an image becomes more complex and intelligent,
availing itself in the first place of the double code dynamics.

Further innovations have emerged also in the field
of the planning phase of exhibition set-up
for art works and high-end commercial products.
For us these architectural spaces have not the function
to "show" the art works any more,
but to "make them live"
in resonance with visitors' global corporeality,
to be intended as embodied mind.

To this purpose the new exhibition systems

are designed starting from the work of art (or from the product)

that widely "propagates" in the available space.

At this point I would like to explain more in detail

 what neuroinformation is.

Neural networks act as model

of all the interactions that take place

among the composing elements

of any physical, biological and social set.

Despite being eterogeneous among themselves,

these elements get connected the one with the other

through the same synaptic logics as biological neurons.

Consequently such elements work as artificial neurons

or neuroinformation,

 of which the events we are observing are made of.

NEUROINFORMATION

All the images we observe

are elaborated by our brain

as if they were moving

even though they are still in reality,

like those of a painting or of a design object.

This latent dynamics is triggered

by the composing elements of the image

which interact one with the other,

progressively settling the state of their connections

as far as the point of modifying even the initial meaning of

what we are looking at.

In fact if we elaborate any image

according to the paradigm of neural networks,

we discover that it functions

like an evolving dynamic system.

Reserving the explanation of the extent of such process for later,

now let's distinguish this new research trend

from the one similar to Neuroaesthetics,

which studies the visual cerebral areas (Zeki)

and mirror neurons (Rizzolatti).

By using the functional magnetic resonance (fMRI)

these researchers are monitoring

the brain reactions of those who observe some works of art

with the aim to discover the meaning of those paintings .

But in their general work plant

some critical factors nestle,

starting from the most evident one

which regards an implicitly eye-centred conception of art (Zeki).

This limit has been by-passed

by the discovery of mirror neurons, though (Rizzolatti),

which are activated not only through the visibility

of the stimulus, but also through its movement.

Having this new theory been developed

through the analysis of macaques' behavior,

it tends to conceive movement

only as an elementary motoric activation

(i.e. grabbing, biting, beating, giving, etc.)

even when humans are acting.

The kernel of these studies is really challenging, though :

whenever we see someone else doing an action,

in our brain are unconsciously excited

 the same neurons activated in his brain.

As a consequence, the meaning of the action done by someone else

is immediately understood by us at a glance.

If that action is emotionally connoted

(for example crying, applauding, expressing disgust)

then intensive "empathy" is triggered between

who does the action and who observes it.

For example, the perception of somebody else's pain

involves the same areas of the cerebral cortex

that are activated when we ourselves feel the pain.

The discovery of these relational modalities,

surely useful for the treatment of some psychopathologies

such as autism, is not however sufficient

to analyse the relation between

the work of art and the observer.

The main reasons of such inadequacy are three:

a)   as this theory conceives the movement only

under a biological point of view as a motoric act,

other dynamic aspects of art are not taken into account,

as, for example, the materials used in the work of art,

or the energy that deploys in some natural scenarios.

We therefore could not understand why we are attracted

by the energetic lash of a colour or by the charm of a dawn;

b)   even the actions appropriate for such theory,

like for example pushing, cutting, beating etc,

turn out to be however inadequate art wise,

because they are acquired in their original natural form

rather than in the one elaborated by the language of art.

No wonder then, if the works brought to support such theory

are those ones that show the physical gesture of the artist

impressed in the work like a fingerprint (e.g. Fontana's cuts),

or the dynamics of architectural shapes

which mime the movements of the human body,

summarized by Mallgrave

in terms of " tension versus relaxation";

c)   even the emotions, which constitute the nucleus of such research

turn out to be generally flattened,

not only because deprived of their underlying activation process,

(limit due to MRI device, though),

but also because they are segmented in a taxonomic way,

(joy versus sadness; attraction versus disgust etc,),

with the consequent contraction of their natural propagation.

As a result of such simplification of human feelings

we will never be able to understand

the sense of tears of joy (Mirò)

or Mona Lisa enigmatic smile (Leonardo).

In conclusion, this research, still in progress,

has so far only identified which cerebral area is excited

by a determined aesthestic stimulus,

but without having discovered either what happens in that area

or what that activation means.

However, they may be more useful to a neurophysiologist

who locally researches more and more detailed

cerebral circuits, than to an artist or an art user,

interested in discovering possible invariable structures

in the universal language of beauty.

But the paradigm of neural networks

has not been created as a solution

to the issues of the neuroaesthetic research,

because it is specialized

to simulate with a calculator

the functioning of "all the complex systems",

of physical, biological, social, economic

and communicative order.

In conclusion, we can say that this paradigm is based

on the extraordinary connective capacity of our brain,

which is able to activate continuous- flow synapses

among a hundred billion of nerve cells.

Thanks to its hyperbolic connective capacity,

it then becomes a candidate itself as a model

of all the interactions that take place

among the composing elements

of any physic, biological and social set.

Though heterogeneous among themselves,

these elements get connected

with the same modality as biological neurons,

therefore they become virtual neurons in full.

In other words all the information,

a natural or cultural phenomenon is composed of,

functions as artificial neurons.

But what syntax does neuro information combine with?

The answer is simple and astonishing at the same time:

the informative units of any configuration

get connected according to

the " quantitative weight"

they acquire within their own system.

More precisely the weight of a piece of information

is not established by its observer

but by the other information of the same configuration,

which, by getting connected with that unit,

"excite it" with an intensity equal to the sum

of connections activated.

This calculation is fixed

according to the following mathematic formula:

$$W_{ij}(t+1) = W_{ij}(t) + \Delta W_{ij} \quad \text{dove} \quad \eta(t) = \eta 0 \, \exp(-t/\tau)$$

As a result of it, the information which has acquired most weight

within its own configuration,

emerges "earlier" than the other,

that either gets activated later or stays "inhibited"

below their activation threshold.

In this way the structural dimension of time

breaks into the spatial concept of the image,

by using the law of connective weights

to make information emerge in sequence.

The image becomes therefore

"a dynamic system in evolution",

as we asserted at the very beginning of this work.

But within neural networks

the law of connective weights

is not applied only to visual language.

Discovered by neurophysiologist Hebb in his studies

 about the synaptic functioning of our brain ,

this principle has then been extended to all natural phenomena

as universal expression of life,

which mirrors in the functioning of human brain.

Obviously we are not talking about the theory of the whole,

but about a dynamic principle submitted to several restrictions:

a) this principle, in fact, does not generate the simple units of the systems

but it "assembles" them in order to form more complex structures.

For example, the water molecules, studied by Chemistry,

become interesting for neural modelling

only when they get connected with each other and form a wave,

that is a visible undulatory movement;

b) the information of any configuration

is "automatically processed" by our brain,

therefore it reaches our conscience threshold with difficulty.

Someone speaks about unconsciousness to explain such automatism,

but the Freudian unconsciousness is a petty thing

compared to the complexity of automatic knowledge.

In fact while unconsciousness is generated by the "repression", which is achieved by the subject

urged by external causes (rules, prohibitions, expectations, etc.),

the automatic processing, instead,

is freely triggered

by inborn impulses of our organism,

intended as embodied mind.

For example, who of us can ride a bike not for this reason is

able to explain to others how he can keep his balance;

the same thing happens at the supermarket

when we manage to jostle out of the gymkhana of shopping carts

without realizing how we could do it.

The same automatism springs into action also

when we observe an art work.

How many times we have happened to gape

in front of a painting without knowing the reason why;

on the contrary, other times we have happened to neglect

a work of art considering it irrelevant

for the same very instinctive reason.

In conclusion the neural networks demonstrate how

these sensations of ours are not simple

fortuitous suggestions, but the outcome

of an automatic elaborating processing

which is carried out on the basis of latent logic,

different but not less rigorous than the rational one.

Now, if we locate this "automatic intelligence"

in the neural networks modelling,

we discover that it features three innovative specifications

compared to the former psychological knowledge:

a) as it is not regulated by conscious thinking,

    but only by the principle of connective weights,

    this intelligence can be specified as " self- generating process"

    both in the field of physical systems

    and in the biopsychic and communicative ones.

    According to this endogenous dynamics,

    nature can generate a flower or a shell

    just like an artist can intuit an unprecedented form

    or like the observer of the work can feel

    unforeseen and intense sensation.

    In other words, the way nature gets organized

    is "homeomorphous" to the synaptic one

    of our automatic thinking.

    As a consequence the self- generating process of dynamic systems

    implies a change of paradigm

    in the humanistic conception of creativity.

    The latter, in fact, can no longer be conceived as individual inspiration

    but as the expression of "collective intelligence"

    which makes use of deep biopsychic mechanisms

    common to all individuals.

    Being therefore generated by nature,

    this collective intelligence is wider and more articulated

    than the homonymous one of computer science,

    which is restrained to "big data"

produced by the only users of the net,

who, in addition, are brought to perceive reality

according to the abstract categories

of the symbolic systems.

b)   this automatic intelligence also avails

itself of feed-forward techniques,

which project forward the automatic elaboration of information

towards advanced evoluting stages.

Infact, it avails itself of the contexts where inputs are

to drive their elaboration towards unpredictable results.

Not very different was also the physiological evolution of our cerebral apparatus:

archaic, limbic, neocortical.

c)   inputs are interactively elaborated

by man's all cerebral systems.

Despite their having distinct functions,

these three cerebral systems, infact, work in

tight dynamic connection,

so as to increase our cognitive potential

at the highest possible level.

These three cerebral systems of mankind,

despite having different functions from each other,

they, however, work in tight dynamic connection

so that to increase our cognitive potential

at the highest possible level.

But this sophisticated natural machine

is tacitly sabotaged by our cultural models

which, due to different historical reasons,

do not exploit all mankind's cerebral functions.

Now, let's better analyse this issue.

Western culture, founded since its origins

on the Neocortical predominance of knowledge,

is focused on abstract symbolic representations,

such as the word and the logical formalism of the calculator,

which, on the contrary, are less relevant in Oriental culture.

This gap between the two systems of reality representation

has been stigmatized by Lyotard in a famous statement:

" When Western people speak, Oriental people dance".

We have to admit, though, that the Western culture,

by making the most of this very limited cognitive modality,

has, however, succeeded in promoting science and progress

in all the fields of human knowledge.

But in its laudable opening towards all fields of knowledge

it has, however, " parcelled" cognitive dominions

by creating fences among disciplines

also within one same area.

It's the drama of modernity!

Of little use have therefore been the excellent examples

of the interdisciplinary research

by an Edelman, Nobel prize winner for immunology,

who has studied the conscience;

by a Barrow, an astrophysician, who has discovered

the biological basis of beauty;

by an Atlan, a biophysician, who has described

the self-organization of the meaning

in cellular automata.

As minor examples we could quote also the collaborations

among experts of different disciplines

committed in the implementation of the same research project.

The interdisciplinarity is therefore the pillar

of the new frontier of knowledge.

This cognitive turning point has been already

stigmatized by someone with a sensational sentence:

"The doctor who knows everything about medicine

knows nothing about it".

In the field of humunastic culture

this spread of knowledge is getting itself established

as a contamination among images, sounds,

theatre, cinema, architecture and dance.

But this polifonia of expressive forms does not go beyond

the semiotic competence of the person who, for example,

is able to speak 10 languages ignoring though

the language of the body.

Obviously also this semiotic competence

can reach a higher level of complexity

when it starts an interaction with scientific dominions

(physics, mathematics, biology, informatics and neuropsycology).

At this point the real meaning of interaction

between cognitive symbolic and sub-symbolic systems springs into action.

And this is the very specific and constitutive trait

of the neural networks paradigm,

which is spreading in the more advanced countries,

involving different sectors of knowledge:

- the modelling of artificial vision (Edelman, Wenshall, Poggio)
- the anthropomorphic robotics (Picard, Cingolani)
- the architectural design (Watanabe)
- the financial markets forecasts (Chaos Management, Stoccarda, Parigi, Atlanta)
- the bio-artificial intelligence (Langton, Parisi)
- the endogenous language of the objects and visual arts (Colecchia)
- other sectors of knowledge characterized by the co-existence of order and chaos.

In each of such sectors the modelling of neural networks

has made relevant innovations,

such as those reached in the classical visual arts,

design and exhibition systems.

The main discoveries achieved

in my laboratory, Synapticart, are three:

the method for information processing,

the double code of the aesthetic message,

the energetic resonance between the configuration of the art work

and the global phisicality of the user.

Let's describe these points in their order:

METHOD: the visual configurations are worked out

through a "bottom-up" process, i.e. proceeding from bottom to top.

According to this new research methodology,

in order to interpret any work of art

you don't start from a general set of knowledge

(history, culture and symbols),

but you arrive at them starting from

the physical, perceptive and functional aspects of the work,

that is from the matter.

From this main methodological approach two consequences come out:

- the analysis of the matter implies the fine-tuning

  of a micro analytical instrument

  based on notions of physics, biology and neuropsychology.

  The use of this tool makes emerge

  from the deep layers of single works,

  unknown aspects and contents for the current experts in the field,

  who still use the traditional perspective.

  Of course in this case the comparison

  is not to be made among the individual researchers,

  but among their tools of analysis.

  The prescription glasses in fact

  are somewhat different from the electronic microscope!

- Under the action of this magnifying glass

  the work unveils the hidden genesis

  of its own "intrinsic meaning",

  which gets organized into a sub-symbolic

  narrative sequence.

  But what do we intend by "intrinsic meaning"?

While symbolic systems "represent" reality

with formal unities out of it

 (the word, infact, takes the place of the object),

the sub-symbolic language, on the contrary,

 "shows directly" the internal structure of things,

identifying it through physical

and connective weights principles.

As these principles are identical to

the synaptic ones of our brain,

the meaning of what the sub-symbolic language expresses

 can be automatically understood by everybody,

because it is not represented by external codes.

From this stems the definition of intrinsic meaning

as internal self representation of reality.

THE DOUBLE CODE: the work of art, meant as a dynamic system,

emits physical signals and symbolic units

configured into two codes:

under the semiotic code, which is of stylistic

and historic-cultural nature,

which belongs to our official culture

acts a sub-symbolic one of biopsychic nature,

which emits physical micro signals, never detected so far.

They are connective patterns, hidden units,

proprioceptive impulses, cerebral noise, motoric schemes,

inborn motivational systems, oscillatory movements,

energetic resonances, dynamic attractors,

distributed and parallel representations, etc.

The whole of these items constitutes the natural grammar

of the "sub-symbolic language" of the neural networks.

As this language is inborn,

it can be automatically produced and understood

by all individuals

regardless of their national, cultural, educational variables,

which act though in the above symbolic level of the work of art.

It is necessary, then, to specify that in Western culture,

based on abstract symbolic representations,

the inborn expressive modalities of mankind,

such as instinct for example, have been inhibited.

Therefore we have to take back

the automatic intelligence (intuitive, sensorial and motoric),

ghettoized by present cognitivist theories.

THE ROLE OF THE BODY: being the work of art a dynamic system,

it interacts with the global physicality of the user

at a level of deep "resonance"

like the one between two energetic systems.

In fact the work of art and the user's body

are configured like two oscillatory systems,

of which one is formed by physic micro signals

of sub-symbolic language,

whereas the other is formed by the expressive manners

of human body, meant as embodied mind.

For the first time, therefore, the observer's body

breaks into the mediatic scene as the generator and elaborator

of the deep and pervading sense of the art work.

This new body language is projected

beyond the current performing experiences of "body art"

and the multisensorial expressive systems.

The set of innovations described so far

has been tested on many works of art

belonging to great artists of

ages and places very different the ones from the others :

Leonardo, Mirò, Magritte, Chagall, Beuys, Brewster, Weston,

Kutner, Gehry, Piano, Cattelan, Quinn, Hirst and others.

They have fine-tuned intuitively, that is automatically, sub-symbolic

expressive mechanisms hidden underneath their stylistic and

historic-cultural configurations of their works.

Being inborn these mechanisms have determined an undisputable

success of such works in every age and place.

Also in the design field

the neural platform has produced

radical innovations on three fundamental levels of planning:

a) the needs and the expectations

of potential users of the design product

have been detected by using the

"inborn motivational systems" (IMS) of behaviors.

This model has made neuropsychological meanings come to light,

which were beneath the detected needs at sociological level

or through the direct involvement of users (Design Thinking).

b) the fine-tuning of a strong and original design image,

is achieved according to precise phases of process,

which range from Thom's "morphogenesis"

to the sub-symbolic language and from this

to energetic resonance.

c)   by interacting with the global physicality of the user,

the design object has unveiled

an array of biopsychic functions

interconnected the ones with the others in a network.

In this new research prospect

A chair which is useful only to sit down,

can't even perform that !

These scientific innovations

have found surprising validation in the latent,

structural matrixes

of great designers ' masterpieces,

such as Mendini, Maurer, Pesce, Stark, Gehry,

Ferragamo, Zanotti, Rossetti and others.

Designing their own artefacts

these artists have given the impression to exactly sticking

to the specific criteria of the neural networks,

they had no cognition of, though.

No wonder!

The sub- symbolic language of neural networks

is in fact a"natural language" emerging

from the abyss of the embodied mind.

Being so unlimited, the abyss doesn't belong to

the artist's individual subjectivity any more

but to human species' as a whole.

It is this the innovative sense of biopsychic

concept of "collective intelligence", which distinguishes

from the homonymous one of informatics.

The latter is infact based on big data

provided only by the users of the net,

who express themselves

 through the abstract categories of verbal language.

These data show also the disadvantage

of not being correlated to the contexts, to the inborn

motivational systems of users.

Through the same scientific platform,

also Exhibition Systems have been designed

to display art works in museums, galleries and exhibitions.

Such spaces are not conceived any longer

to "make the art works be seen",

but to "make them be lived",

in resonance with visitors' global physicality,

meant as embodied mind.

The crucial points of such exhibition set up are:

- the exhibition system is designed starting from the art work

    that propagates at wide spectrum in the surrounding space;

- this space is configured as an architectural bubble,

    which receives the visitors in small groups

    to involve them in a plunging experience into art ;

- the work in fact narrates the genesis

of its own artistic, semantic and emphatical configuration;

- the contents of such narration propagate

  onto the concave surface of the bubble,

  but in surprisingly different forms

  from the ones expressed contemporarily by the work.

- these different signals, though,

  are intertwined with the ones of the art work

  at biopsychic level,

  according to the principle

  of the "parallel and distributed representations"

  of the neural networks.

Let's ask ourselves why

this new research trend should be considered

better than the others.

The answer entails the following points:

a) we live in a complex society, which raise the problem of comprehension

   among people of different tastes and cultures.

   The sub-symbolic language of neural networks,

   by operating underneath the conventional language systems,

   opens up an automatic understanding channel among strangers,

   who can so exchange "signals of biopsychic nature".

b) the sub-symbolic language of neural networks

   opens up an unprecedented scenario in the communication science.

   Infact, it " no longer represents" reality with symbolic units external to it,

   (the symbol replaces the content)

   but "shows it directly" identyfing the internal structure of things, on the basis of the principles of physics

and the connective weights.

As these principles are similar to the synaptic ones

of our brain, the meaning of what is expressed by the subsymbolic language

can be automatically understood by everybody,

without the classic mediation of the codified languages :

the machine language, that of the interfaces

and the internet of things.

In this way the innovative endogenous language of objects was born,

discovered in my laboratory Synapicart.

c) also the "holistic" character of the neural networks

can produce innovative effects on the present separation

of disciplinary knowledge,

which represents the drama of modernity.

Infact, this allows to overcome the old and new dichotomy

as the one between

-   body and mind
-   nature and culture
-   matter and symbol
-   hardware and software
-   artificial and biological intelligence
-   order and chaos

These brief research clues

might also be furtherly endorsed

by the opinion expressed on the neural networks

by the great mathematician Strogatz,

reaffirmed in Italy by Odifreddi:

" The neural networks are the first unitary model of complexity

ever appeared in the history of scientific research.

It is a cutting-edge theory,

which explains why nature, society, economics and communication

work alike, that is according to dynamic principles

typically appropriate of nature".

Bibliography

Al-Khalili J. e McFadden J.   (2015)   **Life on the edge. The Coming of age ofQuantum biology**, Wiedenfeld & Nicolson Ltd, London

Anderson P. W. e Stein D. L.   (1997)   **Broken Symmetry**, Addison-Wesley, Redwood City

Arbib M.   (2012)   **How the brain got language**, Donald Loritz, OUP, USA

Argan G. C.   (1984)   **Arte e critica d'arte**, Laterza, Bari

Argan G. C.   (2009)   **Promozione delle arti, critica delle forme, tutela delle opere. Scritti militanti e rari**, A cura di Claudio Gamba, Marinotti Edizioni, Milano

Atlan H.   (1987)   **Self creation of meaning**, Physica Scripta, 36, 356

Atlan H. and Koppel M.   (1990)   **The cellular computer DNA: program or data**, Bull. of Mathematical Biology, 52, 335

Berline D. E.   (1974)   **Study in the new experimental aesthetic**, Wiley, New York

Bertoz A.   (2013)   **La Vicariance, Le cerveau créateur de monde**, Odile Jacob, Paris

Bertuglia A. e Vaio F.   (2013)   **Complessità e modelli**, Bollati Boringhieri, Torino

Barrow J.D.   (1995)   **The Artful Universe**, Oxford University Press, New York

Bistagnino L.   (2011)   **Design sistemico**, Slow Food Editore, Bra

Boulez P. e Changeaux J. e Manoury P.   (2016)   **I neuroni Magici**, Carocci Editore, Roma

Caglioti G.   (1994)   **Simmetrie infrante**, Città Studi Edizione, Milano

Celant G.   (2011)   **Arte Povera**, Mondadori Electa, Milano

Chaitin G. J.   (1975)   **Casualità e dimostrazione matematica**, Le Scienze, 85

Clark A.   (1999)   **An embodied cognitive science ?**, Trends in Cognitive Science, 1, 345-351

Clark A., Chalmers D. J.   (1998)   **The extended mind**, Analysis, 58, 7-19

Colecchia N., Zaccardi F.   (2000)   **La rottura della simmetria nella comunicazione visiva**, FrancoAngeli, Milano

Colecchia N.   (2016)   **Anatomy of a painting**, Amazon.com

Cross N..   (2011)   **Design Thinking**, Berg Publishers

Damasio A.   (2000)   **Emozione e coscienza**, Adelfi, Milano

Darwin C.	(1872)	**The expression of emotion in man and animals**, Murray, London
Dehaenes S.	(2014)	**Coscienza e Cervello, come i neuroni codificano il pensiero**, Cortina, Mi
Di Nuovo S.	(2013)	**Autonomous Learning in humanoid robotics through mental imagery**, Neural Network, 41, 147-155
Di Nuovo S.	(2014)	**Prigionieri delle neuroscienze?**, Giunti Editore, Firenze
Edelman G.	(1989)	**The remembered present : a biological theory of consciousness**, Basic Books, New York
Edelman G., Tononi G.	(1998)	**Consciusness and complexity**, Science, Vol. 282
Edelman S., Weinshall D.	(1989)	**A self-organizing multiple view representation of 3/D objects**, Technical Report at Memo, 1146, CBIP Memo 41, Cambridg, Mit Press
Ekman P., Oster H.	(1979)	**Facial Expression of Emotion**, Ann. Rev.Psychol, 30
Floreano D., Keller L.	(2010)	**Evolution of adaptive behavior in robots by means of Darwinian selection**, PLoS Biology, 8, 1
Gallese V., Freedberg D.	(2007)	**Mirror and canonical neurons are crucial elements in esthetic response**, Trends in Cognitive Science, 11, 411
Gauchet M.	(1994)	**L'inconscio cerebrale**, Nuovo Melangolo
Golubitsky M., Field M.	(1995)	**The symmetry in chaos**, Oxford University Press, Oxford
Hebb D. O.	(1949)	**The Organization of behavior**, Wiley and Sons, New York
Hickok G.	(2015)	**The Myth of Mirror Neurons: The Real Neuroscience of Communication and Cognition**, Amazon Kindle
Jacobson R.	(1966)	**Saggi di Linguistica generale**, Feltrinelli, Milano
Kimbell L.	(2009)	**Beyond design thinking**, L. Kimbell, PE Street, CRESC Conference, Manchester
Kohoenen T.	(2000)	**Self Organized Formation of topologically correct feature maps**, Biol.Cybern, 43-59
Kolmogorov A. N.	(1965)	**Tree Approaches to the quantitative definition of information**, Problem of Information Trasmission, 1, 4
Kurzweil R.	(2005)	**The Syngularity Is Near**, Viking Press, Penguin Group, USA
Langton G.	(1989)	**Artificial Life**, Addison Wesley, Redwood City
Le Doux J. E.	(2002)	**Synaptic Self**, Viking Penguin, New York
Liotti G.	(1986)	**La dimensione interpersonale della coscienza**, NIS, Roma
Lumier L., Zeki S.	(2011)	**La bella e la bestia**, Laterza, Roma-Bari
Maffei L.	(1995)	**Arte e cervello**, Zanichelli, Bologna

Mallgrave H.F.	(2015)	**L'empatia degli spazi,** Raffaello Cortina Editore
Mandelbrot B. B.	(1982)	**The fractal geometry of nature,** Freeman, San Francisco
Mandelbrot B. B.	(2001)	**Nel mondo dei frattali,** Di Renzo Editore, Roma
Marr D.	(1982)	**Vision: a investigation into the human rappresentation and processing of visual information,** W.H. Freeman, San Francisco
Norman D. A.	(2004)	**Emotional Design,** Basic Books, New York
Parisi D.	(1999)	**Mente. I nuovi modelli della vita artificiale,** Il Mulino, Bologna
Parisi D.	(2001)	**Simulazioni,** Il mulino, Bologna
Parisi D.	(2006)	**Origins and evolution of language,** Oxford University Press, Oxford
Poggio T.	(1991)	**L'occhio e il cervello,** Edizioni Teoria, Roma
Poggio T., Edelman S.	(1990)	**A network that learn to recognise 3D objects,** Nature, 343
Ramachandran V. S., Hirstein W.	(1999)	**The Science of Art : a neurological theory of aesthetic experience,** Jounal of Consciusness study, &, 15-51
Ritter H., Martinez T., Schulten K.	(1992)	**Neural computation and self-organizing maps,** Addison-Wesley, Redwood City
Rizzolatti G.	(2005)	**The Mirror neuron system and imitation.** In Hurley S., Chater N. (a cura di) Perspectives on Imitation, From Neuroscience to Social Science, MIT Press, Cambridge (MA) vol. 1, 55-76
Rizzolatti G., Sinigallia C.	(2006)	**So quel che fai. Il cervello che agisce e i neuroni specchio,** Cortina, Milano
Rosemblum L.	(2010)	**See What I'm Saying. The Exstraordinary Powers of Five Senses,** Amazon.com
Rovelli C.	(2014)	**La realtà non è come ci appare. La struttura elementare delle cose.,** Ed Cortina Raffaello
Smale S.	(1980)	**The Mathematic of time,** Springer-Verlag, New York
Stern D.	(1982)	**Le prime relazioni sociali: il bambino e la madre,** Armando, Roma
Thom R.	(1985)	**Modelli Matematici della Morfogenesi,** Einaudi, Torino
Vettese A.	(2006)	***Capire l'arte contemporanea,*** Allemandi, Torino
Watanabe M. S.	(2006)	***Induction Design,*** Universale di Architettura, Torino
Weiskrantz L.	(2001)	**Coscienza perduta e ritrovata: un approccio neuropsicologico,** Mondadori, Milano
Zamataro L.	(2007)	**Il computer emozionale. Coscienza, emozioni, cibernetica,** Bonanno, Acireale-Roma
Zeki S.	(1993)	**A Vision of the brain,** Blackwell, London
Zeki S.	(2009)	**Splendors and Miseries of the Brain, Love, Creativity, and the Quest for Human Happiness,** Wiley-Blackwell, London

Printed in Great Britain
by Amazon